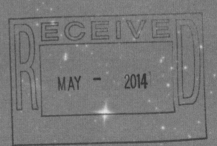

How to Make a Planet

A Step-by-Step Guide to Building the Earth

Written by Scott Forbes   Illustrated by Jean Camden

Kids Can Press

For Ruari, Jamie, Lara, Hayden, Minnie Bo and Mal

Kids Can Press edition 2014

First published in Australia in 2012 by Weldon Owen Limited

© 2012 Weldon Owen Limited

Kids Can Press acknowledges the financial support of the Government of Ontario, through the Ontario Media Development Corporation's Ontario Book Initiative.

Published in Canada by
Kids Can Press Ltd.
25 Dockside Drive
Toronto, ON M5A 0B5

Published in the U.S. by
Kids Can Press Ltd.
2250 Military Road
Tonawanda, NY 14150

www.kidscanpress.com

Concept and Project Manager Ariana Klepac
Text Scott Forbes
Design Mark Thacker, Big Cat Design
Consultant Jack Challoner
Illustrator Jean Camden, Hackett Films

KCP edition edited by Caitlin Drake Smith

IMAGE CREDITS

JEAN CAMDEN, HACKETT FILMS: cover, 1, 3 (bottom right), 4, 6–7, 8 (bottom), 9 (right), 10 (top left), 11 (bottom), 12–13 (bottom center), 13 (top right), 14 (bottom left), 15 (top and bottom left), 16 (top), 17 (bottom right), 19 (top), 20 (top), 21 (bottom), 22 (top and bottom left), 23, 24 (top), 25, 27 (top), 28 (top), 29, 30 (top right), 31 (top and figure bottom), 32 (top), 33 (bottom right), 34 (bottom left), 35 (left), 37 (left), 38 (left), 39 (bottom), 40 (top), 41 (top right), 42–43 (top center), 43 (right), 44 (top), 45 (bottom), 46 (figure bottom center), 47 (top right), 48 (bottom), 49 (top), 50 (top), 53 (bottom), 54 (top), 55 (bottom right), 56–57 (figures and chart bottom), 58 (figure left), 59, 60 (left), 61 (right)

SHUTTERSTOCK: all other images

This book is smyth sewn casebound. Manufactured in Shenzhen, China, in 10/2013 by C & C Offset

CM 14 0 9 8 7 6 5 4 3 2 1

Library and Archives Canada Cataloguing in Publication

Forbes, Scott, author
   How to make a planet : a step-by-step guide to building the Earth / written by Scott Forbes ; illustrated by Jean Camden.

Includes index.
Originally published: Sydney : WeldonOwen, © 2012.
ISBN 978-1-894786-88-1 (bound)

   1. Earth sciences — Juvenile literature. I. Camden, Jean, illustrator II. Title.

QE29.F67 2014   j550   C2013-903958-9

Kids Can Press is a *lorus*™ Entertainment company

CONTENTS

So, You Want To Make a Planet?

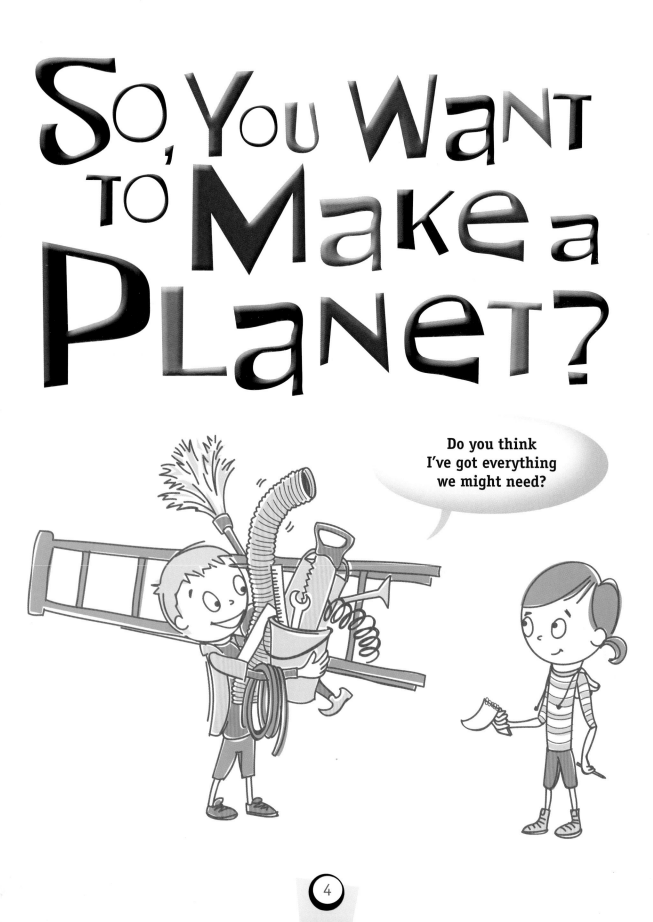

Do you think I've got everything we might need?

Okay! **What's the best way to understand something complex or technical?** Take it apart, or try to make it yourself. To help you understand your world, this book is going to show you how to make a planet, just like the one you are standing on. Using the latest scientific experiments, discoveries and calculations, it will tell you exactly what you need to gather and how to stick it all together to create an appealing, life-supporting, Earth-size ball of rock, complete with oceans, land, plants, animals and smart, attractive humans just like you.

Some of it just might be a little bit difficult to achieve in the average home living room — okay, downright impossible. But what can't be done can still be imagined, and by reading this book, not only will you find out how Earth, our home planet, came about and learn many, many remarkable things about it, but you will also start to appreciate what an incredible, one-in-a-billion (or more!) kind of place it is.

Are you ready? Let's go!

Time from Big Bang	What's happening	Years ago
0		13.7 billion
1 second	Microscopic particles form	13.7 billion
3 minutes	Protons and neutrons start bonding	13.7 billion
20 minutes	Protons and neutrons stop bonding	13.7 billion
380 000 years	First atoms form. Space now transparent.	13.69962 billion
200 million years	First stars appear	13.5 billion
700 million years	First galaxies take shape	13 billion

Bit of a wait here ...

9 billion years	Planetary system forms	4.7 billion
9.1 billion years	Our rocky planet takes shape	4.6 billion
9.17 billion years	Planet's solid metal core forms	4.53 billion
9.31 billion years	Hard crust forms	4.39 billion
9.4 billion years	Atmosphere forms. First life-forms appear.	4.3 billion
9.5 billion years	High rainfall creates oceans	4.2 billion
9.7 billion years	Thicker continental crust forms	4 billion
9.9 billion years	Lava flows increase thickness of crust. Fewer comet and meteor bombardments.	3.8 billion
10.2 billion years	Oxygen-producing life-forms appear	3.5 billion
11.3 billion years	Oxygen levels rise in atmosphere. Ozone layer forms.	2.4 billion
12.7 billion years	First multicelled life-forms	1 billion
13.26 billion years	First animals and plants appear on land	440 million
13.35 billion years	High oxygen levels help animals grow bigger	350 million
13.5 billion years	Animals now widespread on land	200 million
13.695 billion years	Ape-like creatures evolve	5 million
13.6998 billion years	Human species (*Homo sapiens*) exists	195 000
13.7 billion years	Our planet as we know it!	TODAY

WAY TO GO!

EXTREME! Putting a planet together will take you on the ride of your life. Here's a time line of how it happened for our planet, Earth, to use as a guide.

Begin with a Bang!

BOOM! To get off to a flying start, you need a bit of a bang. Actually, a really, really *Big Bang*. One that will send lots of stuff flying all over the place and create powerful forces that will eventually join that stuff together. It has to start very small and grow unimaginably big, and it has to be so strong that it will go on for billions and billions of years — enough time to make your planet.

SQUISH! First of all, you'll need to gather every bit of energy and matter in the universe — absolutely *everything,* in other words — and squish it all down to something about a thousand times smaller than this dot. Yep, that one at the end of the last sentence. Not only our planet, but our entire universe, started off that small.

Around 13.7 billion years ago, all energy and matter were compressed into a minuscule, superhot speck that you would have great difficulty seeing even with a powerful magnifying glass. There was *nothing* else, no space or sky, outside it. Everything was contained in that point. Wow!

LET iT RiP!

All at once, the point expanded at an incredible rate. In a split second, it was the size of a grapefruit, an instant later 1 km (0.6 mi.) wide. Within a minute, it was billions of kilometers/miles wide. It has been growing ever since. Today, the universe is so large we can't even see its edges with the most powerful telescope on Earth, never mind reach them.

LiGHT-YEAR

To describe enormous distances, scientists use the light-year, which is a measure of the distance that light — the fastest thing in the universe — travels in a year. A single light-year is the equivalent of 10 trillion kilometers (6 trillion miles) — that's 10 000 000 000 000 km or 6 000 000 000 000 mi. — and our universe is many *billions* of light-years wide. Yep, that's *big*.

BiG NUMBERS

Putting a planet together involves some pretty large numbers, so you'd better get your head around them now.

- A *billion* is a thousand million: **1 000 000 000** (a 1 followed by nine zeros).
- A *trillion* is a million million: **1 000 000 000 000** (a 1 followed by twelve zeros).

To save time writing all those zeros, scientists use a shortcut, inserting a little number after a 10 to indicate the number of zeros. So a hundred is 10^2, a trillion is 10^{12} and so on.

Keep squishing! We've got to get everything down to the size of a tiny dot!

The most distant object ever seen is a galaxy 13.2 billion light-years away from Earth.

LISTEN UP!

Yeah, right, you might say. Earth and everything else came from a tiny speck?! Where's the proof? Good question. Part of the answer is that we can still "hear" the Big Bang. In 1964, two American scientists, Arno Penzias and Robert Wilson, were using a huge radio telescope when they noticed a constant background hiss and crackle coming from space. Eventually, Penzias and Wilson realized that what they were hearing was caused by heat radiation from the Big Bang, which was still spreading across the universe — as it continues to do today.

FAR-OUT!

Another part of the answer to your question is that we can see the effects of the Big Bang, too. Peering through giant telescopes, scientists have noticed that, in every direction they look, the galaxies (big groups of stars) farthest away from Earth keep moving farther and farther away. This can only be happening if the universe is expanding.

As a bright spark like you will have quickly worked out, that means the farthest-away objects are the oldest. The most distant object ever seen is a galaxy 13.2 billion light-years away. That means it is 13.2 billion years old and its light has taken 13.2 billion years to reach us. So we are seeing it as it looked when the universe was just 500 million years old!

THINK AHEAD Will the universe go on expanding forever? Many scientists think it will. Eventually that could mean that the stars spread out so much that they run out of energy, causing all life in the universe to die out. Don't worry, though! If that happens, it will be many billions of years — maybe 10^{33} years — in the future.

CRUNCH! Other scientists have suggested that in billions of years the universe may reach a maximum size and start collapsing, shrinking and shrinking until, once more, it is just a tiny dot — an idea known as the Big Crunch. And then it might all begin again, with another Big Bang.

So, keep squishing. Get all that stuff down to the right size, and we'll get on our way!

Hey! I think I've discovered a new galaxy!

START YOUR CLOCKS

TICK TOCK

As soon as the Big Bang lets rip, you can start your clocks and watches. Time has begun! And if all goes well, some amazing things will start to happen. Blink, though, and you will miss them.

WAIT A SECOND!

In the first microsecond, tiny particles called quarks will be whizzing around, crashing into one another at terrific speed. But as your universe expands, it will also start to cool. And, as the temperature drops the teeniest fraction, the quarks will slow a little and start bonding together in groups of three to form new particles called protons and neutrons.

Then, before your watch has even clicked off a single second, a whole lot of other particles will have appeared, including trillions of really minute ones called electrons.

Time Check

1 second
- *Universe already 1 km (0.6 mi.) wide!*
- *Billions of fast-moving particles*
- *Super hot — ouch!*
- *Dark — you'll need a flashlight!*

CRASH TESTS

You might not manage to recreate the Big Bang in your living room, but scientists today are trying to do something similar in research centers, using huge machines called particle accelerators. The largest of these is the Large Hadron Collider near Geneva in Switzerland. Something like a giant circular pipeline, it occupies a 27 km (17 mi.) long tunnel 90 m (295 ft.) underground. It blasts protons together at tremendous speed in an attempt to split them into quarks and reveal more about conditions at the time of the Big Bang.

Hey, did you know that temperature is actually a measure of how fast particles are moving? When a gas expands, its particles slow down, and so the gas cools. That's what happened to the universe after the Big Bang!

Proton

Neutron

Hurry up! We've only got 17 minutes!

PAIR YOUR PARTICLES

Within 3 minutes, with the temperature now down to a toasty 1 billion degrees Celsius (1.8 billion degrees Fahrenheit), the protons and neutrons will slow down and start combining, in a process called nuclear fusion. This forms tiny clumps of up to four protons and four neutrons.

They'll have to hurry up, though! Scientists have worked out that during the Big Bang, protons and neutrons had *only 17 minutes* in which to get together! After that, with the temperature falling quickly, it just wasn't hot enough for nuclear fusion to continue.

WHAT'S THE MATTER?

So, after 20 minutes you'll have some protons and neutrons that have bonded, but most will still be flying around on their own. One proton or a group of protons and neutrons forms what's known as a nucleus (plural: nuclei) — the very beginnings of any substance. A single proton is the nucleus of a substance called hydrogen, and at this point, hydrogen nuclei will make up around three-quarters of all the matter in your universe.

Almost all of the rest of the universe will be nuclei of helium, each made up of two protons and two neutrons. There will, however, also be tiny amounts of another form of hydrogen, called deuterium (one proton and one neutron), and minuscule traces of lithium (three protons and three neutrons) and beryllium (four protons and four neutrons).

And that's it! A great swirling mass of these substances, mixed with countless neutrons and even tinier electrons, is all you will have for quite some time — hmm, roughly 380 000 years or so. Yes, it sounds like an eternity, but it's the blink of an eye in planet-making terms. So hang on in there!

> The force that draws positive and negative electrical charges together is called **electromagnetism.**

Awesome!

Time Check

20 minutes

- *Wow, the universe is now trillions of kilometers/miles wide — mostly made up of hydrogen and helium nuclei*
- *Countless electrons whizzing around*

Helium atom

MAKE SOME ATOMS

Around 380 000 years later, things will have settled down a bit, the temperature will have dipped to a balmy 2700°C (4900°F) and your particles will have slowed down further. This will allow the electrons, which have a tiny negative electrical charge, to start bonding with the protons in the nuclei, which have a tiny positive electrical charge (neutrons have no charge). When the electrons and protons join together, the momentous result is — drumroll, please — the atom!

What's so exciting about that, you say? Well, atoms are the building blocks of absolutely everything. So this is a pretty big moment. If you've got this far, pat yourself on the back.

IN NEUTRAL

Inside an atom, the nucleus is at the center, and the electrons — there are usually the same number of electrons as there are protons — whirl around the nucleus. The electrons are held in place by the attraction between their negative charges and the protons' positive charges. These charges cancel each other out, so an atom is neutral.

ELEMENTARY!

The simplest substances are made up of only one kind of atom and are known as elements. At this point, your universe will contain just four elements — hydrogen, helium, lithium and beryllium, with hydrogen still making up three-quarters of all material and helium most of the rest.

But eventually, more complex mixtures of protons, neutrons and electrons will provide you with a whole load of other interesting elements, including other important gases such as oxygen and nitrogen, metals such as gold and iron, and nonmetals such as sulfur and chlorine.

TOP OF THE CLASS

It's the number of protons in an atom that determines what kind of element it forms, and this is called its atomic number. For example, hydrogen has one proton, helium two, lithium three and so on. The Periodic Table — there's one on the wall of most school science classrooms — is a table of all the elements, arranged by atomic number. So hydrogen is number 1 in the table, helium number 2, lithium number 3 and so on.

Hydrogen atom

SUDDEN SWITCH

So, atoms ... not impressed yet? Just wait till you see what they can do! Of course you won't see them at all because they're so extremely tiny. And you'll have to give them a bit of time to really get going. How long? Well, at least 200 million years or so. Time enough to look up and take in the view. For something has suddenly changed.

BECOMING CLEAR

Up to now, all those charged particles, especially the negatively charged electrons, have been getting in the way of particles of light, or photons. As a result, the universe was opaque — meaning you couldn't see through it.

But now that the positive and negative charges have joined together in atoms, the light particles can do their thing and stream around here, there and everywhere. So all at once the universe has become transparent — see-through — and everything is a little bit clearer. It might not look too impressive: just a gloomy expanse barely lit by a tangled but evenly spread web of light. But, hey, at least you can see it's there!

SO SMALL

Just as scientists use scientific notation for huge numbers, so they also use it for tiny numbers. For example, 0.0001 can be written as 10^{-4}. Think of the 4 as the number of digits after the decimal point, or the number of zeros plus a 1. So 10^{-20} is the same as but a heck of a lot neater than 0.00000000000000000001. Atoms are approximately 10^{-12} m (3×10^{-12} ft.) in size. Another way to think of them is that you could fit several million of them on a pinhead.

Time Check

380 000 years

- *The first elements form. Cool!*
- *Universe has become transparent*
- *If you look very hard, you can see a faint web of light*

BRING ON THE STARS

TURN ON THE LIGHTS

For many millions of years, you'll be looking at a murky, gaseous expanse, wondering if anything is *ever* going to happen. But if you look carefully, you'll notice that, slowly but surely, changes are happening — thanks to gravity.

Gravity is the force that pulls objects together, usually smaller ones toward larger ones, like you toward the ground when you fall over! In your new universe, slightly denser areas of gases will gradually form. These areas will exert a stronger gravitational force than the areas around them and will therefore start to draw material in. Over millions of years, as they become thicker still, their pull will strengthen, and the process will speed up.

IN A SPIN

Smaller, denser clouds will then appear inside these areas. And, about 200 million years after your Big Bang, some of these smaller clouds will collapse in on themselves and start to spin, creating an effect like water going down a drain — a bit like a whirlpool.

As the atoms at the center of a cloud like this are pressed together, they'll move faster and the temperature will soar. Once it reaches a scorching 10 million degrees Celsius (18 million degrees Fahrenheit) or so, nuclear reactions will take place, releasing huge amounts of energy. Then the center of the cloud will glow white-hot and — presto! — a star will be born.

Time Check

200 million years

- *Murky clouds of gas everywhere*
- *Hooray! The first stars appear!*

Types of stars

White dwarf

Main sequence star (like the Sun)

Wow! That red supergiant is BIG!

Red giant

Red supergiant

LIVES OF THE STARS
All stars form this way, but they grow to different sizes and live for different lengths of time. Larger stars generally use up their energy more quickly and therefore have shorter lives.

NEBULAE
The cloud that gives birth to a star is called a nebula (plural: nebulae). Usually, it takes about 40 million years for a nebula to grow to a fully formed star, which is then known as a main sequence star. A main sequence star will normally stay in tip-top condition for 10 billion years or so.

GOING OUT WITH A BANG
As it runs out of energy, a star starts to swell to up to 40 times its previous size, pulsate and glow orangey red, at which point it's called a red giant, or a red supergiant if it's really big. A few billion years later, it sheds its outer layers, creating another gas cloud and leaving behind a little cooling core called a white dwarf, which will hang around for billions of years.

Occasionally, however, an old star — usually one that is very big and still has lots of energy — will go out in a blaze of glory: a colossal explosion known as a supernova.

GATHER MORE INGREDIENTS

All this spinning, igniting, burning and exploding will produce a heap of new substances. And some of these will come in very handy for your new planet.

STAR POWER

In the intense heat caused by stars forming, larger numbers of protons, neutrons and electrons will come together to create new elements: oxygen, carbon, neon, iron, nitrogen, silicon, magnesium and sulfur. And as giant stars explode, even more elements will be scattered across the universe. Some of these will be gases, but some will take the form of specks of dust — the universe's first solid particles!

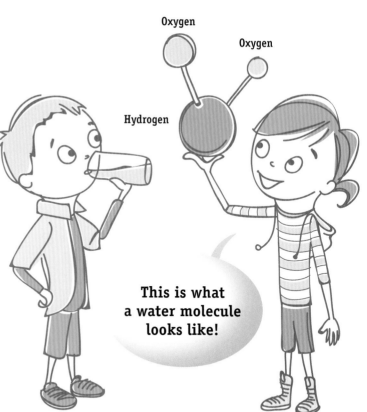

Oxygen

Oxygen

Hydrogen

This is what a water molecule looks like!

SNAPSHOTS IN SPACE

Because a star's life cycle is so vastly long, no one ever gets to see the whole thing. But star formation is taking place all the time, so we *can* see stars at all stages of life. In the famous constellation Orion, for example, we can see a nebula where stars are currently being born, main sequence stars and even a red supergiant.

HANGING OUT

Even more awesomely, different kinds of atoms will start hanging out together, getting on brilliantly and bonding to form new structures called molecules. And different combinations of atoms in molecules will create more and more substances. For example, when two hydrogen atoms team up with an oxygen atom — hi, guys! — you get water. From here on, the possibilities are endless!

Most of the 90 or so naturally occurring elements on Earth are thought to have first formed during the birth or death of stars!

CHECK OUT YOUR STAR

The star you'll be most familiar with is the one that lights up your life: the Sun (yep, the Sun is a star). A fairly average main sequence star, the Sun is about 1 392 000 km (865 000 mi.) in diameter — more than 109 times the diameter of Earth. Like all stars, the Sun uses up energy at a phenomenal rate — about 550 million tonnes (600 million tons) of hydrogen *per second* — but luckily it has plenty in reserve. Don't worry. It'll be another 5 billion years or so before it even reaches the red giant phase. So chill out!

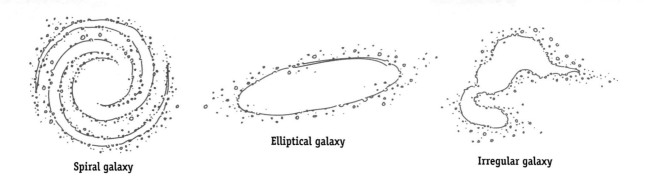

Spiral galaxy

Elliptical galaxy

Irregular galaxy

COMPARE YOUR GALAXIES

One by one, those stars will light up your universe. Soon, you'll see that some gas clouds have given birth to hundreds or thousands of stars — groups known as clusters. And some of the biggest clouds will contain humongous collections of millions or even billions of stars, called galaxies.

Time Check

700 million years

- *Stars scattered right across the universe*
- *Look, the first galaxies are starting to take shape!*

WHEELING AROUND

Galaxies form in three main shapes: spiral, elliptical and irregular. Spiral galaxies, shaped like great pinwheels in the sky, usually have a bulge at the center and long rotating arms of gas and dust where new stars are forming. Elliptical galaxies are ball- or oval-shaped and contain mainly older stars and little fuel for new star formation. Irregular galaxies are normally fairly small and have no clear shape.

MILKY WAY

The Sun is one of about 100 billion stars in a spiral galaxy we call the Milky Way. Look up on a clear night and you'll see the white, fuzzy band of stars that gave it its name. The Sun sits not at the center of the galaxy but out on one of the arms of the spiral, the Orion Arm.

As galaxies go, the Milky Way is a pretty big one, measuring about 100 000 light-years in diameter. If you could travel across it in a spacecraft like NASA's *Voyager* probes, which can travel at up around 17.3 km (10.7 mi.) per second, it would take you 1.7 billion years! Wow!

BLACK HOLES

At the center of most galaxies is a black hole, a massive, incredibly dense object. So powerful is its gravitational pull that nothing that moves close to it can escape, not even light — and, as you will remember, light is the fastest thing in the universe. That's why black holes are black — there is no light!

TIME TO TAKE A BREAK

Though the all-star action is now nonstop, it may be some time before the conditions are just right for your planet to start taking shape. How long? Well, it could be several *billion* years. Okay, it's probably time to have a bit of a rest!

Scientists think that any object that goes near a black hole would be sucked in and stretched into long, thin strips before being obliterated. This is known as spaghettification!

Um, I think we should move out of the way of this stellar nebula!

step 4 WHiP UP SOMe PLaNeTS

FEELING REFRESHED?

Great! While you've been dozing, billions of stars and galaxies have gone on forming, shining and dying. Now, about 9 billion years on from your Big Bang, it's time to start checking those stars more closely. Look carefully and you may find that some are surrounded by a whirling disk of dust and gas. If so, it could be the start of something!

STIR SOME DUST

The disk of dust around a star is called a stellar nebula. Inside this spinning mass, it will be chaos! Billions of solid particles will be whizzing around, glancing off and smashing into one another.

Gradually, some rocks will stick together and grow bigger until they form whirling 1 km (0.6 mi.) wide rocks called planetesimals. And a few hundred thousand years later, some of these planetesimals will merge to produce massive lumps called protoplanets — baby planets, in other words. Aww, how cute!

HOT AND COLD

Any protoplanets that form near your star will be too hot to retain gases, water or ice, and will therefore be mainly rocky, like Earth. A little farther out, however, large balls of gases may form around small rocky cores. And even farther away from the star, the planetesimals and protoplanets will be made mainly of ice. Brrr!

Time Check

9 billion years

- *Big cloud of dust and other bits of matter are spinning around a star now*
- *You can see planetesimals and protoplanets starting to form in the cloud*

AROUND THEY GO!

As full-size planets form, they will settle into orbits around the star. They will all move in the same direction and all on the same plane, or level. It's a bit like a huge, slow-moving carousel!

WHOOSH! When the star reaches its full size, it will emit a blast of energy called a stellar wind. This will sweep away most of the remaining dust and gas, leaving behind a fairly neat and tidy set of orbiting planets or, as we call it, a planetary system. It might play havoc with your supercool hairstyle, though!

GET TO KNOW YOUR NEIGHBORHOOD

Our own planetary system, the solar system, formed more or less in this way, about 4.6 billion years ago. The rocky planets — Mercury, Venus, Earth and Mars — took up orbits close to the Sun. Debris and rocks that didn't become planets gathered in a band called the asteroid belt, just outside these four rocky planets. Collisions between these rocks, or asteroids, sometimes send them flying off across the solar system. Watch out!

What's in a Year?

The time it takes a planet to orbit its star is called a year. The farther from the Sun a planet is, the longer its orbit and the longer its year. Earth takes 365.25 days to orbit the Sun, giving us a year of 365 days and an extra day every four years (each leap year). On Mercury, the planet that has the shortest orbit, a year is just 88 Earth days — not so long between birthdays, in other words. Meanwhile, way out on Neptune, a year lasts almost *165 Earth years*. So you wouldn't even reach your first birthday there!

Time Check

9.1 billion years
- *Planets starting to take shape now*
- *Planets moving into their orbits*

GAS PLANETS

Beyond the asteroid belt, the gas planets — Jupiter, Saturn, Uranus and Neptune — spread across a huge area. These planets are called "gas giants" because they are made mostly of gas and are much bigger than the other rocky planets. Each gas giant has a small, dense, rocky core.

HEY, PLUTO!

Even farther out, a much smaller frozen lump, known as Pluto, does a good impersonation of a planet. So much so that when it was discovered in 1930, it was thought to be our ninth planet. But in 2006, astronomers decided Pluto didn't make the grade and is just one of many small protoplanets still surrounded by debris. Poor Pluto.

Pluto

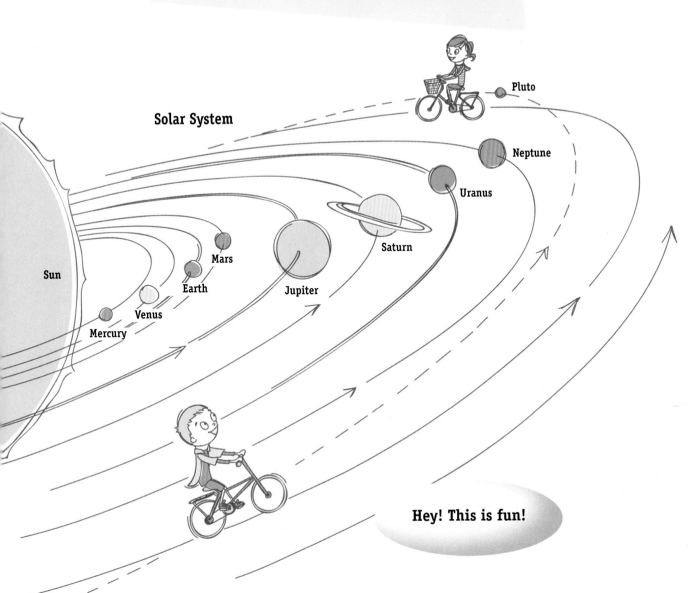

Solar System

Pluto

Neptune

Uranus

Saturn

Jupiter

Mars

Earth

Venus

Mercury

Sun

Hey! This is fun!

WAY OORT Thousands of other icy planetesimals are thought to orbit in a vast band beyond Neptune, known as the Kuiper Belt. And outside that, and surrounding the entire solar system, is the immense Oort Cloud, which is full of trillions of icy objects of various sizes, orbiting the Sun at all angles. You wouldn't know it, but it's pretty busy out there!

These areas are the source of comets, lumps of ice and dust that sometimes drift into the inner solar system. If a comet moves close to the Sun, it appears in the sky as a bright light with a tail made of ice that has vaporized from the comet as it nears the Sun, and dust released as the ice vaporizes.

The average distance from Earth to the Sun is 150 million kilometers (93 million miles). Astronomers call that an astronomical unit (AU). Neptune is about 30 AU away and Proxima Centauri is 271 000 AU away. Extreme!

PLAN A TRIP? Now that you've got your bearings, you might be keen to plan a space vacation. But before you pack your suitcase, you'd better give some thought to how far and for how long you might have to travel.

SLOW COACH The Moon, a mere 385 000 km (240 000 mi.) or so away, is as far as any astronaut has ever gone. If you could travel there in a car, keeping up a steady highway-like speed of 100 km/h (62 m.p.h.), it would take about 160 days — more than five months — to arrive and unpack your picnic blanket. At that same speed, it would take more than 45 years to reach the nearest planet, Venus, which at its nearest is just 38 million kilometers (24 million miles) away.

EXPRESS SERVICE

It'd be much better to take a spaceship, of course. Astronauts reached the Moon in three days. In 2005–2006, the pilotless *Venus Express* got to Venus in 153 days, around five months. Not too bad. But what if you wanted to head farther out, away from the Sun?

Launched in 1977, the pilotless *Voyager 1* and *Voyager 2* probes travel at up to 17.3 km (10.7 mi.) per second. Even so, it took them more than three years to reach Saturn (1.4 billion kilometers or 870 million miles away) and eleven years for *Voyager 2* to reach Neptune (4.5 billion kilometers or 2.8 billion miles away). Hmm — better put that Saturn summer vacation plan on hold.

And if you're aiming for the stars, forget it. The Sun's next-door neighbor

SPOTTING STARS

Astronomers are constantly scanning the skies for other planetary systems that may be like ours. A few hundred planets that orbit other stars have been spotted. Most are giant gas planets like Jupiter, rather than rocky Earth-like places. We'll just have to wait to find out if they are as special as your planet!

is Proxima Centauri, an old, smallish, faint star. It's about 4.22 light-years away, which doesn't sound like a big deal, until you remember that's almost 40 trillion kilometers (25 trillion miles). Or 40 million million kilometers (25 million million miles) — 40 followed by 12 zeros (25 followed by 12 zeros). Go on: try writing out those zeros.

If *Voyager 2* were to continue at its current speed to Proxima Centauri, it would arrive after ... wait for it ... 73 000 years!

Proxima Centauri 4.22 light-years

Sun 150 million km (93 million mi.)

Neptune 4.5 billion km (2.8 billion mi.)

Many other planets have moons — bodies that orbit around them. Jupiter has 64!

Bake to Perfection

CHOOSE A PLANET

Around 9 billion years after you started, you will have a set of planets spinning around a star. Now you need to pick out one planet as your very own. You want a nice, solid, rocky one, of course. And one that's in just the right place. Choose carefully!

TEMPERATURE CONTROL

Earth is sometimes called the "Goldilocks Planet" because, like the porridge Goldilocks preferred in the story "Goldilocks and the Three Bears," it's neither too hot nor too cold, but just right. This is partly because it's far enough from the Sun to stay cool, and close enough to be warm. But it's also due to the calming influence of our only natural satellite, the Moon.

Time Check

9.16 billion years

* *Our planet now orbiting the Sun*
* *Planet still being bombarded with pesky planetesimals and other debris*

WOBBLY

In its early days, about 4.54 billion years ago, Earth was, like many youngsters, lively but a little unsteady. As it still does, it orbited the Sun while spinning around its own axis — an imaginary line through its center. But it also swung more wildly on this axis, wobbling like crazy as it went.

THWACK!

While still a wobbly infant, Earth suddenly crashed head-on into another, smaller planet, and the cores of the two planets merged. Other debris broke off and began spinning

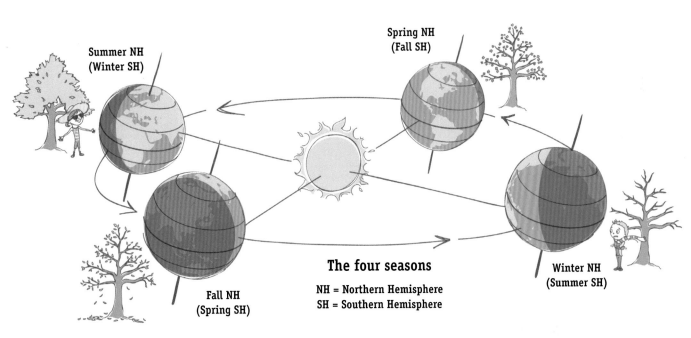

Summer NH
(Winter SH)

Spring NH
(Fall SH)

Fall NH
(Spring SH)

Winter NH
(Summer SH)

The four seasons

NH = Northern Hemisphere
SH = Southern Hemisphere

ON THE BRIGHT SIDE

As Earth spins on its axis every 24 hours, you move from daytime (the side of the planet facing the Sun) to nighttime (the other, dark side). The tilt in Earth's axis creates our seasons. In the middle of the year, the North Pole tilts toward the Sun, so it's warmer (summer, in other words) in the Northern Hemisphere and colder (winter) in the Southern Hemisphere. By the end of the year, the seasons have reversed.

around the newly expanded Earth, and eventually it all stuck together and formed the Moon, which still orbits our planet.

PULLING POWER

The Moon doesn't look like it's doing much up there, does it? No atmosphere, no people, no fun. But though the Moon is much smaller than Earth — roughly one-fourth of Earth's diameter — it still has a big influence. Its gravitational pull not only causes the tides in our oceans, but it also has a steadying effect, reducing Earth's wobble to no more than one degree.

If it weren't for that, temperatures on Earth would be much more extreme, and life — at least as we know it — may never have developed. So next time you look at the Moon, give it at least a nod of thanks.

> Phew! These rocks are pretty hot!

CRANK UP THE HEAT

As your planet takes shape, it will still be colliding violently with rocks, meteors and comets, its interior will be cooking away and most of its surface will still be boiling molten rock. All that's going to make things uncomfortably hot for a while. Hey, don't complain — that's exactly what you want!

HEAVY METAL

When the temperature inside your planet reaches a critical point, the heavier metals will sink to the center and form a solid core like a metal ball. This spinning, superhot ball will then create a magnetic field. And in turn, this will form a radiation shield around the planet that will protect it from dangerous cosmic rays. How nifty is that?!

HAPPY CATASTROPHE

Earth developed an iron core as early as 10 million years after it began to form. Because this event was so huge and violent, scientists refer to it, in a rather gloomy way, as the iron catastrophe. But, cheer up, it's actually a good thing!

TIME CHECK

9.17 billion years

- *Our planet now has a solid metal core*
- *Super hot inside and out*
- *Surface is molten rock — ouch!*

SPACE SHIELD

Earth's magnetic field is what causes the needle on a compass to point to the North Pole. This magnetic field extends thousands of kilometers/miles into space, protecting our planet from harmful solar wind and radiation. If this shield suddenly disappeared, the solar wind would blow most of Earth's water off into space, and life on Earth would have hardly any chance of surviving. Yikes!

ALLOW TO COOL

Over the next 150 million years or so, as more space debris merges with the planets, there will be fewer collisions and your planet will start to cool a little. Gradually, a hard crust will form.

DOWN BELOW

Rocky planets generally have a core of heavy metals, a rocky middle layer made of lighter materials, which is usually called a mantle, and a crust. Earth's core is divided into a solid iron-and-nickel inner core and a liquid iron-and-nickel outer core. Likewise, the mantle has a solid lower layer and a soft upper layer. Its rocks are made mostly of oxygen, silicon and magnesium, whisked together with a little iron and aluminum. The crust is rich in these elements, too, but also peppered with other ingredients such as calcium, sodium, potassium and sulfur.

Radioactive

Many elements inside our planet, such as uranium, are radioactive, meaning that their nuclei break up, or decay, emitting heat as they do so. This "radioactivity" produces up to 80 percent of Earth's internal heat, keeping the planet's insides very toasty.

TEST YOUR CRUST

By this stage, your planet should be reassuringly solid and heavy. And how is that crust coming along? Still warm? Thin, is it? Hard, but a bit brittle in places, you say? Awesome!

THIN-SKINNED

It's about 6400 km (4000 mi.) from wherever you are standing now to the center of the Earth. But, on average, the crust — the ground beneath your feet — is only 34 km (21 mi.) deep. You might imagine it to be like the thick rind on a watermelon, but in fruit terms, it's more like the thin skin of an apple.

9.31 billion years
- *Finally our planet now has a solid crust*
- *Still radically hot inside, though!*

DIG IT?

Even so, no one has ever cut through the crust. Want to have a go? Get out your shovel and start digging. It might be easy at first, but pretty soon you'll hit solid rock. You might try a hammer or a pick then, but what you'll really need is a massive rock drill.

Even if you do manage to borrow one from your neighbor, it will still be very hard work. As you dig deeper, it will get hotter and hotter. Just 3.9 km (2.4 mi.) down — which is the depth of the world's deepest mine, near Johannesburg, South Africa — the temperature will be an unbearable 55°C (130°F). And from there on, it will become between 25°C and 30°C (77°F and 86°F) hotter for every 1 km (0.6 mi.) you descend. Phew!

OUCH!

The deepest hole anyone has ever dug is in Russia. Drilling began in the 1970s, and by 1992, the hole was

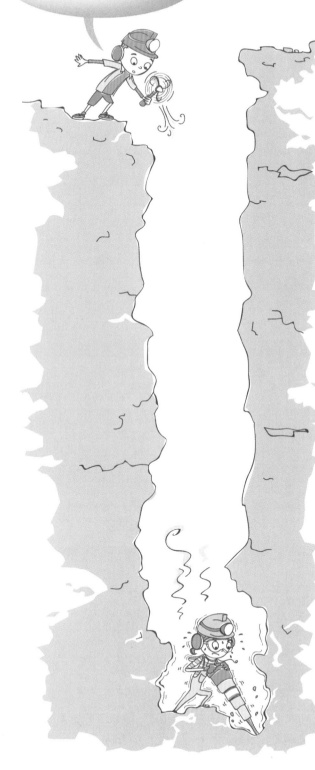

It looks very hot down there!

JOURNEY TO THE CENTER?

If you could actually dig to Earth's center, and moved at the rate of 30 cm (1 ft.) per minute, it would take you about 40 years to get there. Driving a car nonstop at 100 km/h (62 m.p.h.), you'd arrive in less than three days.

12.3 km (7.6 mi.) deep. At that point, work had to stop because the temperature had reached 300°C (572°F) and the drills kept melting. Got the picture?

CHECK THE CENTER

So, if no one has ever got below Earth's crust, how can we tell what's down there? Well, sometimes volcanoes conveniently spew out rocks from the mantle that can be tested in laboratories to work out their contents.

Scientists also study the progress of seismic waves — shockwaves from earthquakes or explosions set off by the scientists themselves — as they pass through Earth's interior. By measuring how fast they move and are deflected, scientists can tell what sorts of materials are down there.

Add a Little Atmosphere

Just Add Water

With your planet cooking away nicely, you'll soon see gases rising through holes in the crust. Now you need to add water to create that warm, moist, steamy environment we living things all love. Whaddya mean, *you* don't?

Simmer and Steam

The intense heat inside your planet will continue to push molten rock up through holes in the thin crust, forming volcanoes and thicker areas of crust. And it will also belch out a range of gases — um, giant planet burps, you could say.

PARDON ME! Yes, burps. Sounds a bit gross, doesn't it? And 4.3 billion years ago on Earth, when these gases formed a thin layer around our planet — our atmosphere, as we now call it — it would *not* have been a nice place to live. As well as water vapor, there were large amounts of carbon dioxide, methane and smelly ammonia — all of which are poisonous to humans — and almost no oxygen. What's more, the surface temperature was over 100°C (212°F) — way hotter than any human can survive.

Time Check

9.4 billion years

* *A thin layer of gases surrounds our planet. Yay, now we have some atmosphere!*

SPECIAL DELIVERY!
3.3 billion kilograms
(7.3 billion pounds)
of water

HEAT TRAP

Deadly and stinky they may have been, but some of those gases helped form something truly vital. Water vapor, carbon dioxide and methane trapped heat from the Sun close to Earth's surface, keeping the planet warm. This is called the greenhouse effect and it still does its vital job today. Without it, Earth's average surface temperature would be -18°C (0°F). Wow, that's teeth-chatteringly cold!

TOSS IN SOME ROCKS

As well as volcanic eruptions, your planet will still be experiencing regular comet and meteorite impacts. Pretty scary, you might think, but hey, it isn't all bad. These projectiles will be adding some useful ingredients to the mix. On Earth in these early times, icy comets continually deposited huge quantities of oxygen and water as they plummeted to the ground and melted. And what happens when you pour water on something very hot, as your planet will be? Yep, it turns to steam.

BODY OF
WATER

In 2000, astronomers watched Comet LINEAR melt and break up as it neared the Sun. They estimated that it contained 3.3 billion kilograms (7.3 billion pounds) of water — enough to fill a small lake!

Large raindrops that fell in southern Africa 2.7 billion years ago formed tiny craters in volcanic ash that can still be seen today in fossils.

LET iT POUR

Allow your steamy planet to cool further. As the temperature falls, some of the water vapor in the atmosphere will form clouds. Soon, the first raindrops will start to fall. Finally there's some weather on the way!

iT'S GONNA RAIN ...

One day on Earth, about 4.2 billion years ago, it started to rain. And then it kept on raining. Not just for days or a few years, but probably most of the time, and almost everywhere, for thousands and thousands of years. Extreme!

... AND RAIN

This cooled the planet more, allowing water to run across its surface. Soon, torrents of water were thundering down valleys and filling hollows. And as it continued to bucket down, and comets kept dumping additional supplies of water, and Earth kept cooling, water spread across vast low-lying areas, forming the first oceans.

TIME CHECK

9.5 billion years

- *Getting a bit bored with the rain now*
- *Hey, I think the oceans are forming!*

... AND RAIN

Soon, your planet will start to feel pretty soggy, too. But there will still be plenty of heat coming from that red-hot interior. Combined with the heating effect of your star, this will cause some of the water to evaporate (turn from a liquid back into water vapor) and create more clouds and — you guessed it — more rain. Will it never stop?

WATER CYCLE

Well, let's hope not. Because this is what we call a water cycle, and it's still a vital part of our weather today. Water evaporates from oceans and lakes and rises into the air as water vapor. There it condenses to form tiny droplets, which, in large number, create clouds. Whisked here and there by air currents, the water droplets inside clouds collide and merge to form larger droplets. Once these droplets reach a certain size, they tumble out of the sky as raindrops. Then the water runs into rivers and back to the lakes and seas, and the process all starts again.

WATER STORAGE

The larger your oceans grow, the more vigorous this cycle will become. And, as the surface steadily cools, those oceans will eventually become the main driver of weather on your planet.

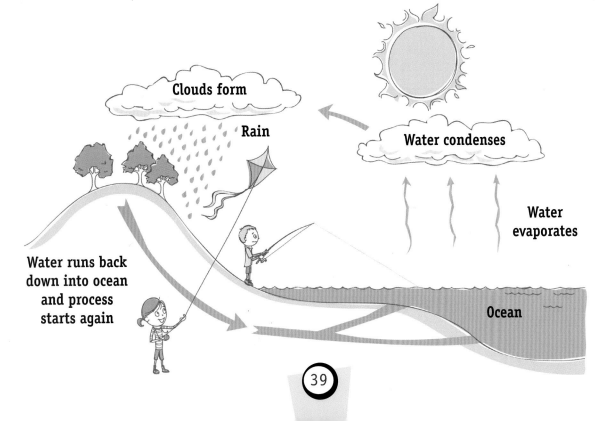

Clouds form

Rain

Water condenses

Water evaporates

Water runs back down into ocean and process starts again

Ocean

SHIFT AND SHAPE

I don't think
I can hold it together
much longer!

CRACKING UP So, now you've got a nice, solid planet with a hard (but thin) crust and a cozy, moist atmosphere. But that crust just won't stay still, will it? It keeps cracking and shifting, pushing some bits higher and plunging others under the sea. Don't get frustrated, though — no, put that glue and tape aside. This is all just part of the process.

Inside your new planet, there's a powerhouse. Heat from the intensely hot core will make the lower part of the mantle hotter than the upper part. This will make the hotter molten rock, or magma, rise toward the surface. There, it will spread out underneath the crust, cool and sink. And then it will be reheated and start rising again. This cycle of rising and sinking magma is called convection.

GIANT JIGSAW

Convection pushes and pulls at the crust, cracking it into large pieces known as plates. That's why your crust will look like a jigsaw puzzle — one that won't stay still! Convection will keep moving the plates around, with some pretty impressive results.

SPREADING
Where heat is rising, Earth's plates push away from one another and the magma underneath seeps through the cracks to form new crust. Under the sea, these cracks are called mid-ocean ridges. On land, they're known as rift valleys.

MOUNTAINS
With plates moving away from one another at one edge, they are going to crash into other plates along their other edges. Where plates collide, a few different things can happen. For instance, two thick plates may crumple up against each other, thrusting land upward. When this happens, mountains are formed.

VOLCANOES
Where a thick plate meets a thin plate, the thick plate (surprise, surprise) usually comes out on top, pressing the edge of the thin plate down into the mantle. However, the thick plate tends to buckle and

Earth's plates move at roughly the rate at which your fingernails grow.

split at the edge. This allows magma to rise up through cracks, creating a chain of volcanoes.

GRINDING
Sometimes plates don't meet head-on, but at an angle. When this happens, the plates slide past one another, moving in opposite directions or the same direction at different speeds, grinding their edges together as they go.

TIME CHECK

9.7 billion years

- *The whole crust is cracked into large pieces. What's happening?*
- *We've got some thicker areas of crust now. Oh, I get it! These are the continents!*

Pangaea

CATCH THE DRIFT

These movements are known as plate tectonics. On Earth, they have been rearranging the continents since soon after the planet formed, constantly changing their shape, position and number.

SUPERCONTINENT

Two hundred million years ago, for example, all Earth's continents were joined together in one supercontinent known as Pangaea. Then they gradually separated and drifted around to form the shapes we know today. Millions of years from now, the continents may look completely different again!

Time Check

9.9 billion years

* *Wow! Huge lava flows are adding to the crust.*
* *At least those comet and meteor bombardments are slowing down now!*

CHECK FOR WEAR AND TEAR

Once that shifting and cracking gets going, you might notice that your crust is changing everywhere — not just at the plate edges. As soon as mountains are thrust up, they start shrinking. Channels appear in the middle of continents. Bits of land slide into valleys and tumble into seas. Whoa! What's going on?!

Shake Well

Where plate collisions occur, we sometimes feel them as vibrations we call earthquakes. About 8000 small earthquakes occur every day on Earth and are hardly noticed. But about 800 large ones rock our world every year. The biggest can destroy buildings, bridges and roads and cause great loss of life.

Continents today

CARRIED AWAY

Winds will also blast rock and blow the dust away. Rain will wash rocks and mud into rivers and carry some to the oceans. Waves will batter the coast, and bits of land will break off and fall into the sea. These kinds of wear and tear are known as erosion.

CRUMBLING

It might look thin, light and fluffy, but your planet's atmosphere can eat through rocks and knock down mountains. The combination of chemicals in your young atmosphere will turn rain and surface water into a mild acid. This acid will eat into the solid rocks, stripping off layers and forming the first soils, muds and sands. At the same time, regular changes in temperature — between day and night, summer and winter — will also cause rocks to split and crumble. This sort of wear and tear is called weathering.

DANGER!

Phew! This ice is hard to shift!

ROCK AND ROLL

Once in the sea, the rocks, mud and sand will sink to the seafloor. Over millions of years, these sediments, as they are known, will pile up, and the top layers will press down on the bottom layers, compressing them into new rock.

The new rock might stay under the sea. Or it might be dragged down into the mantle. Or it might be bulldozed up onto land by plate collisions — and then the atmosphere will start to work on it again. This whole process is called the rock cycle.

The oldest rocks ever found on Earth were discovered in Canada and are 4.3 billion years old.

THE THREE TYPES OF ROCK

All of this is still going on around you every day, and it results in three main kinds of rock. Those that form from the compression of sediments, often under oceans, are called sedimentary rocks. Those that form when lava cools on the surface are known as igneous rocks. When igneous or sedimentary rocks are pushed down into the mantle, they may be scorched and squished so much that they become a different type of rock known as metamorphic rock.

COOL iT!

All this wear and tear is great because it will help create and spread good soils — and make weird and wonderful landscapes for you to enjoy: hills and mountains, rock pinnacles and spires. To assist, make sure there's plenty of water and the temperature keeps changing.

Of course, if you overdo the cooling at any time, you could find that part of your planet freezes. Just allow things to readjust and gradually the ice will melt. That may take a while, though, and the ice will leave its mark.

iCE AGES Earth is known to have gone through several periods of intense cold, usually referred to as ice ages, when much of the land was covered in ice sheets and long rivers of ice called glaciers. The ice sheets smoothed large areas of rock, while the glaciers gouged deep U-shaped valleys that we can still see today.

The first known ice age occurred around 2.4 billion years ago. The last one began 2.6 million years ago and is actually still going on. Oh, hadn't you noticed? Well, today's polar ice caps and glaciers prove it. Though the temperature is quite bearable now,

about 21 000 years ago, ice sheets covered much of northern Europe, Asia and North America, and it was much, much chillier.

We're still living in an ice age that began 2.6 million years ago.

Check for Signs of Life

DOWN IN THE DEPTHS

In your planet's steamy hothouse atmosphere, signs of life will have started to appear, though you may not have noticed. As early as 9.4 billion years after your Big Bang, somewhere down there in those newly formed oceans, the first living things may already have formed.

STIR THE SOUP

And that's pretty amazing, because for a long, long time your oceans will be a deep, murky, boiling hot, toxic soup of chemicals. Ewww! It's hard to imagine that anything could live *there*.

On the other hand, those seas provide protection from many of the hazards on the planet's surface, like comets, lava, dangerous radiation and so on. And the great swill of ingredients down there will result in lots of new substances. So something *could* be brewing. Go on, give it a good stir!

SMALL BEGINNINGS

It's now thought that on Earth, as early as 4.3 billion years ago, chemical reactions deep in the oceans produced the first molecules that could reproduce, or replicate, themselves. The very first

Cells are the building blocks of all life-forms, microscopic parcels that carry and make the chemicals that living things need to survive. You're made up of trillions of them!

Hidden WORLD

It seemed unlikely that life would have first emerged way down in the sea, until the 1970s, when scientists began exploring structures on the ocean floor called hydrothermal vents, where superheated, chemical-rich water rises out of the crust. They found whole communities of organisms thriving down there, despite the lack of light, the intense heat and a mix of chemicals that would kill most other life-forms.

I think I see something by those hydrothermal vents!

self-replicating living things, which appeared soon after, were bacteria made of just one cell — a tiny bag in which these chemical reactions could take place. The bacteria were primitive and nothing much to look at (even through a microscope), but they were alive!

ALLOW TO BUBBLE

Within another 800 million years, as your oceans cool, another type of organism called cyanobacteria should appear near the sea surface. And, if all goes to plan, these bacteria will start to do something that will absolutely transform the planet. Using energy from the Sun, they'll absorb carbon dioxide to make sugar molecules and (this is the vital bit) release oxygen — a trick we call photosynthesis.

Time Check

10.2 billion years

- *Hooray! Finally the planet is cooling down.*
- *Bacteria busy in seas making oxygen*

We can prove this happened on Earth for two reasons. First, because fossilized cyanobacteria have been found that date back 3.5 billion years. And, second, amazingly, because cyanobacteria are still around! In places such as Shark Bay, Western Australia, they inhabit salty bays and form clumps of strange, dome-shaped rocky structures called stromatolites.

PUT UP A SUNSCREEN

The beginning of photosynthesis is a truly magical moment! From here on, the process will slowly but steadily increase the levels of oxygen on your planet. And oxygen is a substance that pretty much all living things require, in one form or another, to survive.

RUSTY

It will be quite some time, though, before there's much oxygen around to breathe. Initially, the oxygen will stay in the oceans and the ground, creating thousands of new minerals, notably compounds called oxides. One of these is iron oxide, which we refer to as rust, and it will start to form on rocks. (You can see these red layers in some ancient rocks today.)

WILD LIFE

There are many way-out theories on the origins of life on Earth. Some people (including famous scientists) have suggested primitive life-forms were sent to Earth by aliens. Others have claimed they arrived on comets or meteorites. That idea may not be so far-fetched, since some meteorites have been shown to contain organic chemicals that are a vital ingredient in life.

Earth's ozone layer formed about 2.4 billion years ago and still protects us today, deflecting up to 99 percent of all ultraviolet radiation. If it weren't there, we'd all get fried!

ON THE RISE
But then the oxygen will start rising into the atmosphere as gas. Some of it will settle between 30 and 40 km (19 and 25 mi.) up in the atmosphere and form a thin but important layer called the ozone layer. This will block ultraviolet radiation (from the Sun) that damages cells, thereby improving conditions for life.

Time Check

11.3 billion years

- *Oxygen levels in atmosphere on the rise*
- *Ozone layer forming — I think it's safe to do some sunbathing now!*

PUMP IT UP
Around 11.3 billion years after your Big Bang, about 0.1 percent of the atmosphere will be oxygen, and 400 million years later, roughly 3 percent will be oxygen. As oxygen levels increase, life will take on new forms. Don't get too excited, though: at this stage, they will still be virtually invisible single-celled bacteria and confined to the sea for another billion years or so.

So, keep stirring.

Those trilobites are cute!

SOFT AND FLOPPY

The first creatures with more than one cell, and the first ones you'll actually be able to see, will appear about 12.7 billion years after your Big Bang. They might look a bit like seaweeds or sponges. Soon after, they'll be joined by other soft, floppy things, perhaps resembling jellyfish.

This is all more exciting than it might seem, for here you have the first mobile, multicelled, food-eating life-forms. Or, as you and I might call them: animals.

HOW DID THEY DO IT?

Just how Earth's single-celled life-forms turned into multicelled ones with bodies, eyes and so on, no one really knows for sure. Maybe some cells started working together, found it went well, high-fived one another and said, "Let's do this again sometime!" and then started getting together in much greater numbers. Or something like that, anyway!

TIME CHECK

12.7 billion years

* *Those oxygen levels are still rising*
* *You can see the first creatures swimming in the sea now. Cool!*

FOSSILS

Whatever the case, we know from fossils that multicelled creatures existed by 1 billion years ago. And that around 550 million years ago, there were suddenly lots and lots of them, especially things called trilobites, hard-shelled creatures that looked like woodlice and ranged in size from as small as a flea to as big as a bicycle wheel.

Trilobite fossil

BE ALERT

If things are going to plan, your seas will by now be teeming with life: jellyfish, fish, water bugs. You've got to keep an eye on things, though, for all it takes is a few overeager volcanoes, a nasty cold snap or a stray meteorite, and — whoops! — most of your life-forms might be wiped out in an instant. Around

440 million years ago, about half of all creatures on Earth suddenly vanished. The most likely cause of this was a sudden, severe ice age, possibly made worse by massive volcanic eruptions.

BOUNCING BACK

If you do find yourself with a major extinction on your hands, don't freak out — it's not the end of the world (well ... probably not). You see, life is tenacious. That means it hangs on and survives where you just wouldn't believe it could, and it keeps looking for new places to live. Pretty soon it will be all over your planet.

APPLY THE FINISHING TOUCHES

LAND, HO!

With life under way, you need to make sure that conditions are right for it to spread far and wide. Sooner or later, some life-forms are going to climb out of those murky seas and head for dry land, where you want them to flourish.

PREPARE YOUR SURFACE

For the best outcome, your continents must have as much rich soil as possible. Of course, you've already got that erosion thing going on, which has created some primitive soils. Even better, the first plants and animals that make it onto land are going to give you a major helping hand.

HERE THEY COME

The first life-forms to emerge from the sea, as was the case on Earth about 440 million years ago, are likely to be algae and miniature mites and bacteria.

The algae will slowly develop into tiny plants, whose roots will help break up that hard, rocky ground.

Meanwhile, the mites and bacteria will also set to work, releasing chemicals into the soil that help break it down, chewing up dirt and plant matter and spitting it out, digging into the ground and, even more helpfully, dying in it. Soon, you'll have your first compost, which plants simply love.

IT'S ALL GOING GREEN

Within a few million years, you'll begin to see larger green shoots popping out of the ground all over the place. Some plants will start producing tiny seeds that will be spread far and wide by winds. Within 40 million years, you might even start to recognize some plants — like ferns.

Time Check

13.26 billion years

- *Ahhhh, nice and humid in most areas*
- *Plants and tiny creatures popping up all over the land*

CREEP AND CRAWL

Meanwhile, slightly larger animals will appear on land, probably millipedes, spiders, some little salamander-like amphibians and insects. You could say it's a creepy, crawly world at this point.

Like cyanobacteria, plants will photosynthesize (absorb carbon dioxide and release oxygen, remember?) and the oxygen levels will continue to rise, helping animals and plants grow bigger.

GIANT BUGS On Earth, about 350 million years ago, during peak oxygen levels, millipedes 2 m (6.5 ft.) long and dragonflies with wingspans of over 1 m (3 ft.) appeared. Glad you weren't around then?

FIND A PLACE FOR EVERYTHING

In another 100 million years or so, trees will sprout and form dense forests. Some amphibians will turn into reptiles, giving you lizards, crocodiles, maybe even dinosaurs, which first began stomping around on Earth about 230 million years ago.

Later, rodents, turtles, crabs and birds will appear. And furry creatures we call mammals. Soon, everywhere you look, things will be buzzing, hopping, slithering and scurrying. Peek into your oceans and it will be teeming with life there, too.

NICHES

Your plants and animals will compete with one another for food and homes, crowd one another out and eat one another. Some kinds, or species, will die out and others will go on and on. Gradually, though, each will find its place, or niche, on land or sea, in the air or under the ground. Eventually, almost every corner of your world will be alive.

Time Check

13.5 billion years

- *Wow, there are grasses, forests and animals appearing! Radical!*

NOT AGAIN!

No matter what you do, accidents keep happening. More major extinctions occurred on Earth about 360 million years ago, killing off one-third of living things; 250 million years ago, when more than 95 percent of creatures died; and, most famously, about 65 million years ago, when a huge meteorite impact is thought to have finished off the dinosaurs, along with half of all other living things.

PREPARE FOR LATECOMERS

After almost 13.7 billion years, it will be pretty much complete, this planet of yours. So, what do you think? What's that? Something missing? Oh, yeah. Hang on. Here they come — at the very last minute.

WAIT FOR US!

About 5 million years ago, certain ape-like creatures in Africa began to walk on two legs rather than four. Various kinds of these hominids — as our earliest ancestors were known — then emerged over the next few million years. But our own species, *Homo sapiens*, did not appear until between 130 000 and 195 000 years ago, in Africa, before spreading into Asia, Australia, Europe and, only 11 000 years ago, North America.

Time Check

13.695 billion years

- *Ape-like creatures appear*
- *Hey, some are walking on two legs!*

AND YOU!

At least 75 000 years ago, humans started drawing on cave walls (it was allowed then). About 10 000 years ago, they began growing crops, and about 8000 years ago, they built the first cities. Next, they started making things out of metal, fighting wars, building houses, making machines and going to schools. Then, you were born, grew up, got up this morning, and now here you are reading this book.

iN A FLASH

It all sounds like a bit of a rush, doesn't it? And compared to all the other stages you have been through in making your planet, the human story really did happen in a flash. Though humans have been around for almost 200 000 years, that's a tiny fraction of the time Earth has existed. And compared to the history of the universe, well ...

A BiG YEAR

Imagine the entire history of the universe, our 13.7 billion years, all squished to fit into one year (grab a calendar: it will come in handy here). Each month will be a little more than a billion years. So, if the Big Bang takes place on January 1, the first stars and galaxies will have appeared by the middle of January. Got that? Okay? So ...

The solar system won't form until late August, and the first oxygen-producing life-forms won't emerge until near the end of September. And even then, life won't really start to flourish till mid-December. The first land-dwelling animals will appear on December 21, and the dinosaurs will show up late on Christmas Day. Early on December 30, they'll be wiped out.

ON THE LAST NiGHT

It won't be until the morning of the last day of the year, December 31, that ape-like creatures will appear, and they won't start walking upright until after nine o'clock — at night.

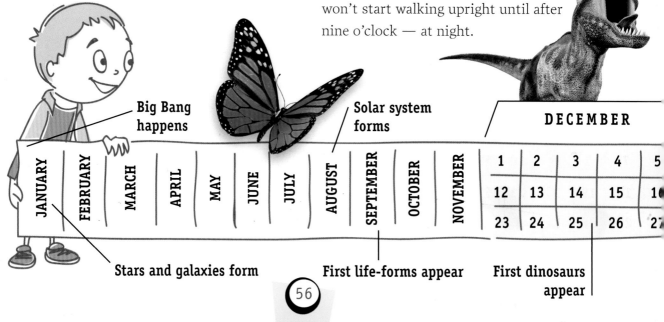

Big Bang happens

Solar system forms

DECEMBER

JANUARY	FEBRUARY	MARCH	APRIL	MAY	JUNE	JULY	AUGUST	SEPTEMBER	OCTOBER	NOVEMBER

1	2	3	4	5
12	13	14	15	16
23	24	25	26	27

Stars and galaxies form

First life-forms appear

First dinosaurs appear

Humans, *Homo sapiens* (that's us!), will finally put in an appearance at about five minutes to midnight. But it will only be in the last 30 seconds of the last minute of the last hour of the last day of the year that they will get started on everything that we call history. (On this scale, Christopher Columbus reaches America about a second before midnight.)

LOOK AROUND YOU

Anyway, you made it, you're here. And that's what counts. Better late than never, as they say! And now you should have a fully functioning planet, complete with plants and animals, clouds and rain, people of all shapes and sizes, dogs and cats, annoying little sisters, crazy dads and so on.

And if *your* planet didn't quite work out, don't worry: you've already got one. One that looks amazing and works beautifully. It's just over there, outside your window. Take a fresh look at it now. It's truly awesome!

Time Check

13.7 billion years

* *Your planet is now complete!*
* *High fives all around!*

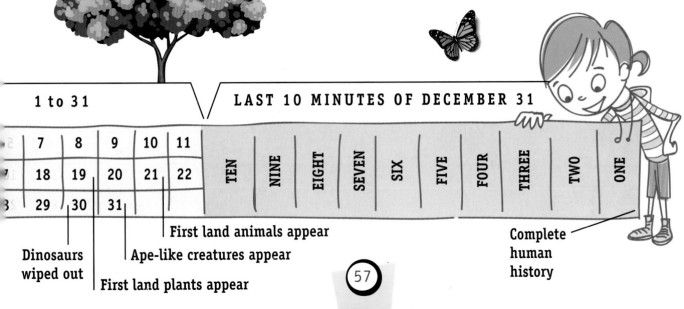

1 to 31

LAST 10 MINUTES OF DECEMBER 31

	7	8	9	10	11	TEN	NINE	EIGHT	SEVEN	SIX	FIVE	FOUR	THREE	TWO	ONE
7	18	19	20	21	22										
3	29	30	31												

First land animals appear

Ape-like creatures appear

Dinosaurs wiped out

First land plants appear

Complete human history

CaRE FoR YouR PLaNET

PHEW! Well, that was quite a job, wasn't it? Billions of years, titanic forces, endless ingredients, careful temperature control, tricky timing, vast quantities of rock, dust, water, glue and tape, and lots of luck. You could probably do with a nap now.

THiNK ABOUT iT Given all that time, effort and good fortune, you'll want to take care of your planet. After all, it's truly amazing that it, and we, exist. Imagine: if it weren't for its perfect location, magnetic field, water-laden comets, the greenhouse effect, the ozone layer — all these things and more — the world you have now might never have taken shape.

ONLY ONE?

What's more, it's not like there is another one nearby. Sure, there *could* be planets like ours in other parts of the universe, but so far we haven't found any with signs of life. And even if we did find a nice life-supporting planet beyond the solar system, right now we'd have no way of getting there.

Good job!

LEARN FROM THE PAST

Better treat your planet well, then. At least, better than humans have treated Earth in the past 150 years or so. In that time, we have been filling the ground and waterways with trash and the air with pollution, cutting down irreplaceable forests and using up huge quantities of natural fuels like oil and coal. Our activities have even started to interfere with some of those amazing natural cycles and processes you've learned about.

TOO COZY!

For instance, human-made chemicals called chlorofluorocarbons (or, if you can't get your tongue around that, CFCs) have damaged the ozone layer. Driving gas-fueled cars and burning coal in factories and power stations have raised the level of carbon dioxide in the atmosphere, making the greenhouse effect (which, as you will recall, keeps Earth warm) stronger and things just a little *too* cozy. If this global warming, as it's known, continues, valuable farmland could dry up, ice caps could melt and seas could rise.

HANDLE WITH CARE

So, do your bit for Earth. Find out how to save energy and reduce waste. Walk or cycle wherever you can instead of asking your parents to drive you. Plant trees. Protect wildlife. Buy Earth-friendly products. Keep your planet tidy. Learn to love your place in space.

And, most of all ... ENJOY IT!

Amazing Facts

OUR PLANET, EARTH

Approximate age: 4.54 billion years

Diameter at equator: 12 756 km (7926 mi.)

Tilt of axis: 23.5 degrees

Rotation time: 23 hours, 56 minutes

Length of year: 365.25 days

Number of moons: 1

Atmosphere: 78% nitrogen, 21% oxygen, 1% water, argon and carbon dioxide

Average thickness of crust: 34 km (21 mi.)

Surface: 70.8% ocean, 29.2% land

Highest point: Mount Everest, 8848 m (29 029 ft.)

Deepest ocean trench: Mariana Trench, 10 920 m (35 827 ft.) below sea level

OUR SATELLITE, THE MOON

Approximate age: 4.54 billion years

Diameter: 3476 km (2160 mi.)

Atmosphere: None

Average distance from Earth: 384 401 km (238 856 mi.)

OUR STAR, THE SUN

Approximate age: 4.7 billion years

Diameter: 1 392 000 km (865 000 mi.)

Composition: 92.1% hydrogen, 7.8% helium, 0.1% other elements

Average distance from Earth: 150 million kilometers (93 million miles; 1 AU)

OUR PLANETARY SYSTEM, THE SOLAR SYSTEM

Approximate age: 4.6 billion years

Diameter: 50 000 AU

Number of planets: 8

Number of moons: 169

Number of asteroids: Millions

Number of comets: Trillions

Largest planet: Jupiter, 11 times the diameter of Earth

Smallest planet: Mercury, two-fifths the diameter of Earth

Nearest planet to Earth: Venus, 38 million kilometers (24 million miles) away (at its nearest)

Farthest planet from Earth: Neptune, 4.5 billion kilometers (2.8 billion miles) away

OUR GALAXY, THE MILKY WAY

Approximate age: 10.4 billion years

Diameter: 100 000 light-years

Number of stars: At least 100 billion

Nearest star to Earth: Proxima Centauri, 4.22 light-years or 271 000 AU away

Brightest star: Sirius, the Dog Star

Biggest star: VY Canis Majoris, 2100 times the diameter of the Sun

THE UNIVERSE

Approximate age: 13.7 billion years

Diameter: At least 90 billion light-years; possibly infinite

Number of galaxies: At least 125 billion

Most distant observed galaxy: 13.2 billion light-years from Earth

GLoSSaRY

asteroids: rocky bodies found mostly in the inner solar system and within the asteroid belt

astronomical unit (AU): the average distance from Earth to the Sun, about 150 million kilometers (93 million miles)

atmosphere: a layer of gases that surrounds an astronomical body

atom: the smallest particle of an element, and the base of absolutely everything

atomic number: the number of protons in an atom

bacteria: microorganisms that live in soil, water, the bodies of plants and animals, or matter obtained from living things

Big Bang: the explosion that caused the beginning of the universe, according to the Big Bang theory

Big Bang theory: the idea that the universe began by rapidly expanding from a superhot and incredibly dense point in which all energy and matter were compressed

Big Crunch theory: the idea that the universe will reach its maximum size and then collapse and shrink until it is just a tiny dot

billion: a thousand million, written as 1 000 000 000

black hole: an invisible region with a very strong gravitational pull believed to exist in space. Scientists think black holes may be caused by collapsing stars.

cell: a microscopic unit that carries and makes all the biological materials that living things need to survive

chlorofluorocarbons (CFCs): human-made chemicals that damage the ozone layer

comets: lumps of ice and dust that sometimes drift into the inner solar system and develop bright tails as they move closer to the Sun

convection: the cycle of rising and sinking magma under Earth's crust

core: the center of a planet

crust: the outer layer of a planet

cyanobacteria: microorganisms that live in water and perform photosynthesis

electromagnetism: the force that draws positive and negative electrical charges together

electron: an atomic particle that carries a negative electrical charge

element: a substance made up of only one kind of atom

erosion: a process where wind, rain and/or waves blast rock until it breaks apart and moves to another location

galaxy: a system of stars and other matter held relatively close together by gravity

gas giants: the four outer planets in the solar system (Jupiter, Saturn, Uranus and Neptune), which are made mostly of gas and are much bigger than the rocky planets

global warming: an increase in the Earth's temperature due to an escalation of the greenhouse effect

gravity: a force that pulls objects together, usually smaller ones toward larger ones

greenhouse effect: the warming of the Earth's atmosphere, caused by heat from the Sun being trapped by water vapor, carbon dioxide and methane in the atmosphere

helium: a light, colorless, nonflammable element

hominids: the family of two-legged, ape-like creatures that includes all humans and their ancestors

Homo sapiens: the human species

hydrogen: the simplest and lightest of all the chemical elements, normally found as a colorless, odorless, highly flammable gas

ice age: a long period of intense cold when much of the Earth is covered in ice sheets and glaciers

igneous rocks: rocks formed when lava cools on the Earth's surface

light-year: a measure of the distance that light travels in a year. One light-year is the equivalent of 10 trillion kilometers (6 trillion miles).

magma: molten rock

mantle: the middle layer of a planet, located between the crust and the core

metamorphic rocks: rocks formed from other types of rock being subjected to intense pressure and heat in the Earth's mantle

microorganism: an organism of microscopic size

Milky Way: the galaxy that contains the Earth, the Sun and the solar system. It is visible in the night sky as a fuzzy white band of stars.

molecule: the smallest particle of a substance that still has all of the characteristics of the substance

nebula (pl. nebulae): a huge cloud of gas or dust in space where stars are formed

neutron: an atomic particle with no electric charge

nuclear fusion: the union of atomic nuclei, which results in the release of enormous amounts of energy

nucleus (pl. nuclei): the central part of an atom, made up of either one proton or a group of protons and neutrons

organism: a living person, plant or animal

oxygen: an element found in water, rocks and free as a colorless, odorless gas. Almost all living things require oxygen to survive.

ozone layer: a layer of Earth's atmosphere that blocks most of the sun's harmful ultraviolet radiation

Pangaea: a supercontinent that was made up of all of the continents of the world and existed about 200 million years ago

particle accelerator: a giant circular machine that blasts protons together in an attempt to split them into quarks

Periodic Table: an arrangement of all of the chemical elements, ordered by atomic number

photon: a particle of light

photosynthesis: the process through which plants use energy from the Sun to absorb carbon dioxide and release oxygen

planetary system: a group of planets and other astronomical bodies that revolve around a star

planetesimals: solid objects about 1 km (0.6 mi.) wide thought to have existed at an early stage of the development of the solar system. They are believed to have collided and merged together to form protoplanets.

plates: large pieces of the Earth's crust that shift and move as they're affected by convection

plate tectonics: a theory describing the shifting of the plates of the Earth's crust. These movements are responsible for the rearrangement of the continents, the formation of mountains and volcanoes, and earthquakes.

Pluto: a protoplanet that was once believed to be the solar system's ninth planet

proton: an atomic particle that carries a positive electric charge

protoplanet: a "baby planet" made of planetesimals that have collided and merged

quark: a small particle believed to make up part of a larger particle such as a proton or neutron

radioactivity: the ability of some elements to give off rays of energy or particles as nuclei within them are broken apart

red giants and supergiants: very large stars with relatively low surface temperatures

rock cycle: the process through which rocks, mud and sand erode into the sea, are compressed into new rocks and either remain under the sea, are pushed onto land by plate collisions or are dragged down into the mantle

rocky planets: the four inner planets in the solar system (Mercury, Venus, Earth and Mars), which are made mostly of rocks or metals

scientific notation: a system of writing numbers as a product of a number between 1 and 10 and a power of 10 (e.g. $7 \times 10^6 = 7\ 000\ 000$), usually used for writing very large or very small numbers

sedimentary rocks: rocks that form from layers of sediment that have been pressed together over time

seismic waves: shockwaves from earthquakes or human-made explosions, often used to study the types of materials below the Earth's surface

solar system: our planetary system, which includes eight planets (Mercury, Venus, Earth, Mars, Jupiter, Saturn, Uranus and Neptune) revolving around one star (the Sun)

stellar wind: a blast of energy emitted when a star reaches its full size

supernova: the explosion of a very large star

trillion: a million million, written as 1 000 000 000 000

trilobites: hard-shelled creatures that looked like woodlice and ranged from the size of a flea to the size of a bicycle wheel. These were some of the first multicelled creatures to exist on Earth.

ultraviolet radiation: harmful rays from the Sun that can damage cells and cause suntans and sunburns

water cycle: the continuous process through which water rises into the air as water vapor, condenses and then falls back to the Earth as snow or rain

weathering: a process where chemicals in the atmosphere and changes in the temperature cause rocks to split and crumble

white dwarf: a small, dense, whitish star that isn't very bright

iNDeX